Sketches Sartorial, Tonsorial and the Like

Sketches Sartorial, Tonsorial and the Like

A collection of light, humorous verse

St. Claire Bullock
Edited by R.V. Andelson

With annotations for the American reader

SHEPHEARD-WALWYN (PUBLISHERS) LTD

First published in 2009 by
Shepheard-Walwyn (Publishers) Ltd
15 Alder Road
London SW14 8ER

British Library Cataloguing in Publication Data
A catalogue record of this book
is available from the British Library

ISBN-13: 978-0-85383-266-6

Typeset by Heavens & Earth Art,
Alderton, Suffolk
Printed and bound through
s|s| media limited, Wallington, Surrey

Contents

Preface

One would naturally assume that *Sketches Sartorial, Tonsorial and the Like* were composed at the very end of St. Claire Bullock's life, but such (save for a few possible exceptions) is demonstrably not the case: "Notes for the American Reader" were found with them among his papers, mainly in the handwriting of his wife (a California native), who died almost two score years before him. This raises the question of why he allowed them to remain unpublished – especially in view of the fact that he depended on his writing for income. While we shall probably never have a definitive answer to this question, nobody who reads the *Sketches* could conclude that it was because he considered them inferior to his published light verse. An unfinished draft accompanying them suggests that he planned to add more poems before consigning them to the press, but was never able to find anything suitable to rhyme with "peplum".

It was long a puzzlement to me why Bullock chose me as his literary executor. After all, he had many distinguished friends who would gladly have served in that capacity. I, on the other hand, was scarcely dry behind the ears – a very junior academic whose acquaintance he had made only a short time earlier.

Recently, I hit upon the answer: Bullock's original literary executor, Albert Heath Chesterfield, predeceased him by seventeen years. His second, William Cutler Bates, predeceased him by fourteen years. His third, Asa Pond, became unable to function in that capacity upon being confined to a mental institution. Aside from my presumed sanity, it must have been precisely because of my youth that he selected me, as providing a greater measure of assurance that I would survive him to perform the office!

This realization brought with it an awareness that I am now in the evening of my life, and that, preoccupied with my own affairs, I had neglected the high responsibility entrusted to me. Therefore, it is with a sense of remorseful urgency that I hasten to make these hitherto unpublished verses of Bullock at last available to the reading public.

R. V. Andelson*
Auburn, Alabama, January 2002

*The late Robert V. Andelson was professor of philosophy at Auburn University, Auburn, Alabama, and an ordained Congregationalist minister. He was the author of several books and numerous scholarly articles.

Master Cecil Abercorn

No wickeder child was ever born
Than Master Cecil Abercorn,
Who, with a pick-axe of his pater's,
Broke in and stole the Bishop's gaiters,*
Then took them to the Cliffs of Dover,
And mischievously hurled them over.

Cast thus upon the roiling sea,
Tossed here and yon as dank debris,
Adrift for many a stormy day,
They finally washed up near Calais.

Some simple fisher folk descried
Them on the shingle at low tide.
Approaching at a cautious creep
These two strange creatures from the deep
(As they first thought them), the good folk
Came timidly to prod and poke,
And, in due course, inspect with care
The Bishop's gaiters lying there.

They pondered long and tediously,
Debating what such things might be,
To no avail, till finally, when
Up spoke the grizzled Luc Duchesne:
"I know now what they are!" cried he,
And bore them home triumphantly.

Each Fall, he fastens them with ease
Around his Pipes so they won't freeze.

*Leggings traditionally worn by an Anglican bishop
(and, on certain occasions, by the dean of a cathedral).

Rupert Ashe

The greatest pride of Rupert Ashe
Was his luxuriant moustache.
He took great care to keep it groomed,
And even, with restraint, perfumed.
He brushed it upward every day,
And it made such a grand display
That people who were not the wiser
Imagined that he was the Kaiser.

The Honorable Cedric Barton

The Honorable Cedric Barton
Admired the Stewart Hunting Tartan.
He came increasingly to covet
A cap or waistcoat fashioned of it.
His scruples would not yield permission
To satisfy this fond ambition,
No Stewart he, or even Scottish,
And so he died morose and sottish.

14

Mrs Stafford Beck

In public, Mrs Stafford Beck
Would drape a fox around her neck.
Although, in fact, the little beast
Was irreversibly deceased,
She named the creature "Antoinette,"
And viewed it almost as a pet.
At home one day when she was ill,
She read the story of *Miss Brill,*
And Antoinette was laid to rest
Forever, in a camphor chest.

*A work by Katherine Mansfield, in which the title character's happy world is
shattered when she overhears two young people ridiculing her fox neckpiece.

Dame Portia Blague

The iron-willed Dame Portia Blague
  Detested humbug like the plague.
  Her sense of honesty allowed her
  No hint of rouge or trace of powder.
She would not deign to tint her tresses,
  Or wear defect-concealing dresses.
In fact, she came, in clement weather,
  To abjure clothing altogether -
Which led the Crown to seek to tame her
By sternly threatening to un-dame her.

Canon Nigel Bowman

The Low Church canon, Nigel Bowman,
Considered clericals too Roman.
In time, the garb that he affected,
This viewpoint more and more reflected.
His linen backwards collars early
Were jettisoned, and then, as surely,
Into the dustbin relegated,
His sober suits, to be cremated –
Replaced (What contrast could be starker?)
With clothes that cried: "A circus barker!"
He sported blazers cut too tightly,
And neckerchiefs that flamed too brightly,
And waistcoats chequered all too boldly,
And rings and fobs that gleamed too goldly –
Which facts illumine like a beacon,
Why he was never made archdeacon.

Sir Burton Bowser

The barrister, Sir Burton Bowser,
Declined to wear a pleated trouser.
It was his custom to declare:
"A pleated trouser I'll not wear."
Yet one day, rising from their seats,
His friends observed him clad in pleats.
In unison they fairly shouted:
"Your rule you have quite plainly flouted!"
He answered with a haughty stare:
"My rule applies not to *a pair*."

Pennfield Brooke

A walking stick with silver crook
Was always borne by Pennfield Brooke.
He fancied, in his innocence,
That it would never give offence.
In fact, he thought it just a touch
Of elegance – not overmuch.
Of course, the man was ostracised
From all the circles he most prized;
For Etiquette's imperious rein
Permits a gentlemanly cane,
At most, a silver band, to hide
The seam, where crook and shaft divide.*

*"The only ornamentation allowable is a plain silver or gold band ... The reason why a band on a crooked Malacca is allowed, is that the cost of a single length of wood is prohibitive. The less expensive sticks are made with a joining which is hidden by the band." Emily Post, *Etiquette*.

Dr Brown

The good professor, Dr Brown,
Taught every day in cap and gown.
His choice of calling was astute:
He did not need to own a suit.

Mrs Wilton Bruce

The stately Mrs Wilton Bruce
Would wear no colour save for puce.
From frock to hat to glove to shoe,
Her total wardrobe was that hue.
Her friends decried, much to her ire,
The monotone of her attire,
But she maintained through thick and thin,
It best set off her hair and skin.
What finally made their carping cease
Were these words from her clever niece:
"However tiresome you think puce,
"Be grateful that it's not *chartreuse*."

Clarence Castle

A cotton night cap with a tassel
Was worn to bed by Clarence Castle.
On bitter nights when he was dozy,
It kept his scalp all snug and cosy;
But when the nights were hot and humid,
It made his scalp all dank and tumid.
Without it, even in the heat,
He thought his night-garb incomplete.

Damon Chadwick

When Damon Chadwick was a boy,
They dressed him like Lord Fauntleroy
In wide lace collars, velvet suits,
And little patent leather boots.
His hair was long, his breeches short,
And other lads of him made sport.
Therefore, today one will find Damon
Garbed like a stable-hand or drayman.

The Very Reverend Chalmers Choate

The Very Reverend Chalmers Choate
Wore his round collars extra high
To hide his sagging, wrinkled throat,
About which he was rightly shy.

Plump were his cheeks, spheric, his head,
And bursting from its wide, white band,
His face, all glossy and well-fed,
Recalled a pudding on a stand.

Mrs Chalmers Choate

The randy Mrs. Chalmers Choate
Of St. Elfrida's deanery,
Besmirched her russet redingote
Whilst in an act of venery.
"We'll buy another," said her spouse,
Who found her randiness quite fetching
So long as it was kept in-house.
(He would not brook promiscuous leching.)
But she withdrew from his embrace,
And was not soothed by his endeavor,
Retorting, "You, I can replace.
A redingote like this one, never!"

Crispin Clay

The costermonger, Crispin Clay.
Was bald as ever bald could be,
So took to wearing a toupee
(Except at home, where none could see).

If Sol blazed forth in bright display,
He often added a topee
To shade his face from burning ray,
And shield his eyes from brilliancy.

In haste, one morning in mid-May,
He dressed himself forgetfully,
And ventured forth in disarray,
His toupee topping his topee.

Linwood Cooley

A languid youth named Linwood Cooley
Was awfully partial to patchouli.
He would have worn it, but his Mum
Deemed it not proper *pour les hommes*.
So languid Linwood languished lowly,
Into his deathbed sinking slowly,
And conscience-stricken (Need you ask it?),
Mum poured patchouli on his casket.

Tobias Deering, Esq.

The agèd squire, Tobias Deering,
Required assistance with his hearing,
So, duly a device procured
That made him never miss a word –

Until, at tiffin over sherry,
One day, he grew quite stationary,
And then, immobile, slowly slid
Beneath the table (Yes, he did!),
And lay there snoring quite genteelly.
(The fact is, he had drunk too freely.)
His household servants, three in number,
Were first agreed to let him slumber,
But, after seven hours had passed,
Concurred to waken him at last.

"Arise!" they called in mounting chorus.
"Please, don't just lie there and ignore us.
"Arise! High tea will soon await you
"To comfort and invigorate you."
They might as well have spoken Erse.
His deafness had returned, but worse!

cont. over ☛

They undertook to prod and shake him,
And finally managed to awake him;
But though they spoke in tones ascending,
He still remained uncomprehending.
Otologists from every nation
Were called, but after consultation,
They left with solemn mien, confessing
The case both baffling and distressing.
So, wrapped in silence all-surrounding,
For months the squire, his bosom pounding,
Bewailed his fate, and sat dejected,
His toilet and affairs neglected

Yet, all the while, his butler, Bailey,
Was brooding on the problem daily,
When, as though from a necromancer,
Suddenly there came the answer:

Lodged deep within the squire's ear trumpet
They found a stale, half-eaten crumpet.

Reginald DeLisle

The noble Reginald DeLisle
Was quite indifferent as to style.
His social status was so grand,
He wore whatever lay to hand,
And then, as certain as the dawn,
Others would ape what he had on.
Once, upon leaving Hatton Hall,
He threw on his wife's paisley shawl.
For some time after, one might see,
Fine gentlemen, two out of three,
In shawls, until, in accents stern,
Their wives demanded their return.

Elspeth

When Elspeth was across the water,
Over a dish of sillabub,
Her hostess's athletic daughter
Proposed an outing to the club.
When she agreed, her friend, Meg Vickers,
Said: "We shall golf if it be fair,
"So don't forget to wear your knickers;*
"If need be, I can lend a pair."

"I *always* wear them," Elspeth said,
"Unless, of course, I am in bed."

*In America, knickerbockers or "plus fours." In England, most
commonly, women's underdrawers (originally those cut like
knickerbockers – i.e., loose-fitting and gathered at the knee).

Sir Percival Fitzgibbon, Bart.

Sir Percival Fitzgibbon, Bart.,
Preferred his hair without a part.
For reasons too obscure to tell,
Into a part it always fell.
Without effect, he tried pomade,
And fruitlessly, a barber's aid.
He wore a cap at night to train
His hair, but it was all in vain.
Eventually, he grew so galled
He shaved his head completely bald.

Fenwick Ford

The absent-minded Fenwick Ford
Possessed a cane that made a sword,
And too, to rest his legs and feet,
Another cane that made a seat.
He kept them under lock and key,
Removed from his vicinity.
His reason was a very strong one:
He feared he might sit on the wrong one.

Chilton Fry

A signature of Chilton Fry
Was matching handkerchief and tie.
The Quality, without a doubt,
Mistook him for a pimp or tout.
No matter! He was viewed as smart
By all whose views he took to heart.

Willie Gibb

At mealtime, little Willie Gibb
Simply refused to wear his bib.
Nurse told his parents, "Let him be.
"The bib is useless, for you see,
"The way Young Master spills his food,
"He'd have to dine entirely nude,
"Or else enveloped in a sheet,
"If we would keep him halfway neat!"

Blanche Gillette

From Musgrave Mansions, Blanche Gillette,
In watered silk adorned with jet,
Observed the world through a lorgnette.

Upon her lap, her Pekinese
Whined piteously, for he had fleas;
She was oblivious to these.

E'er long, they multiplied and spread
To Miss Gillette's unwitting head,
And made her scratch until she bled.

The chemist told her to apply
A mix of turpentine and lye
Each day till Candlemas was nigh.

His treatment worked, perhaps too well:
From pet and mistress the fleas fell –
As did their hair, most sad to tell.

Mary Anne, Viscountess Grange

Distracted, Neville, Viscount Grange,
Forgot to ask his wife to change
For tea time at the country house
Where they were guests, he and his spouse.
Poor Mary Anne, who knew no better,
Appeared in flannel skirt and sweater,
Her tea gown folded in a drawer
(She never sure what it was for).
Her hosts and everyone who saw,
Quite overlooking her *faux pas*,
Allowance made for Mary Anne,
Since she was an American.*

*"At English country houses, women always change from tweeds into tea gowns at tea time, but in America one is apt to take tea or go to a cocktail party in whatever dress one had on for luncheon, and dress afterward for dinner." Emily Post, *Etiquette*.

Elvira Greene

The elderly Elvira Greene
Was always in black bombasine.
She was a spinster, and beside,
For decades had no kin who'd died.
The town was curious to know
For whom she mourned, and thus, although
It was indelicate to ask,
A matron brash essayed the task:
Elvira said, in tones of ruth,
"I mourn for my departed youth."

Ralph Griggs

Since character is all that matters,
Ralph Griggs went 'round in rags and tatters.
Once, at a chophouse in York Centre
Two waiters both observed him enter:
"See that old tramp?" remarked the younger.
"He'd like a steak to sate his hunger,
"But through the bill of fare he'll forage,
"And wind up ordering tea and porridge."
And then, with show of perspicuity:
"He'll not leave tuppence for gratuity!"
His more experienced mate, replying,
Said, "You're too rash in prophesying.
"He may be worth a million proper,
"And can afford to look the pauper."

Harold Willis Hackett

For Christmas, Harold Willis Hackett
Received a velvet smoking jacket
Replete with frogs and silken lining,
And broidered with gold cords entwining.
He was so charmed by all its merit,
He took up smoking just to wear it.

Walter Higdon Hall

The plight of Walter Higdon Hall
Was in his county known to all:
Of boots, his conscience let him own
Only a single pair alone.
When it could yield no further wear,
He meant to buy another pair.
In the first instance, he was faced
With choices: Buckled, plain or laced?
With perforations front or back?
Wingtip or cap toe? Brown or black –
Or maybe even British tan?
The leather, kid or cordovan –
Or common cowhide? But, if so,
Pebbled or smooth? High top or low?
The heels, how high? The soles, how thick?
The clerk entreated him to pick,
But he, not used to choices weighty,
Went bootless till he passed at eighty.

Sir Halford Hayes

Whilst at his diplomatic station
In far Dubayy, Sir Halford Hayes
(An Arabist of reputation)
Became attached to Bedouin ways.
With special reference to attire,
He found a *ghutrah* and a *thawb*,
Together with a loose *abaya*,
More suitable than Western garb.
At length, his foreign service ended,
Returned to dwell on English soil,
He could not bear to let his splendid
Exotic garments mould and spoil;
So he resolved to wear them daily,
Though under leaden British skies.
No arguments could countervail; he
Brushed them off like buzzing flies.
A comment from his Cousin Florence
Made his resolve quite limitless:
She said he looked like Colonel Lawrence*
When in his sheikhly desert dress!

*"Lawrence of Arabia."

Serena Huff

The elegant Serena Huff
In Summer wore an ermine muff.
From many quarters came the word:
"A muff in Summer is absurd!"
But she held she was in the right:
"It's quite correct since it is *White*."

Matilda Hughes

Matilda Hughes of Hairston Mews
Was somewhat portly but not fat;
Her eyes, the iciest of blues,
Obscured by large and ugly hat
Beneath whose shade one might discern
A pair of lips extremely thin,
Set in a line correct but stern,
Above a stiff, imperious chin.
Strangers who saw her in a shop
(Attendants scurrying at her beck),
Were apt to make a sudden stop,
Recalling Mary, *née* of Teck.*

They could not wholly see her face,
But bowed or curtsied, just in case

(Whilst the attendants, much bestirred,
Their surreptitious glances joined
To scan the stock and be assured
That nothing dear had been purloined).

*Queen Mary, daughter of the Duke of Teck and consort
of George V. She was a notorious kleptomaniac.

Infant Jane

The christening dress of Infant Jane
Was cheaply made of cellophane.
Her parents held, to have one made
Of lace, or trimmed in white brocade,
Were quite the action of a dunce,
Since she'd be wearing it but once.

Jasper Joad

A pair of muttonchops bestrode
The ample jowls of Jasper Joad,
And tended strongly to convey
An air decidedly passé.
But when his wife once mildly stated
That sidewhiskers were long outdated,
He took her comment quite adversely,
Responding testily and tersely:
"They keep my dewlaps nicely hidden,
"So spare me from advice unbidden."

Julian Katz

The social climber, Julian Katz,
Affected lemon yellow spats,
Yet did not know why men of breeding
Would not acknowledge him on meeting,
Or why no club, e'en a third-rate one,
Would entertain his nomination
So Julian finally fell to brooding
That left him bitterly concluding,
In a despairing mood mephitic,
That he was shunned because Semitic.

Clarence Albert Kells

The dapper Clarence Albert Kells
Would not have commonplace lapels.
When double-breasted, if one watched,
One'd see that they were always notched,
Whereas, if single, rolled and tweaked
To make them always sharply peaked.
Such were the pains that Clarence took
To give himself a *different* look

Rumford Knox

The Boston banker, Rumford Knox,
Insisted on lisle hose with clocks.
Naught else, he held, could swath his toes
Acceptably, save lisle hose
Discreetly clocked, lest they appear
Either too flash or too severe.
"So said my father. So say I,
"And will say till the day I die!"

In time, the footwear fashions changed,
And Rumford's world was disarranged.
His valet voiced the awful news
In trembling tones, that he must choose:
"Clocks without lisle, or lisle without clocks.
"Such lies the outlook now with socks."

cont. over ☛

But Rumford rumbled in his pride,
"Such compromise I'll not abide!
"Give way an inch on trivial things,
"And soon you're tangled up in strings.
"Then, first you know, you cannot foil it –
"All Christian Culture's down the toilet!
"The line I draw; the gauntlet, cast.
"I shall be steadfast to the last.
"Well fortified with Kellogg's Bran,
"I hold the line for Western Man!"

Legions of servants he deployed,
Yet all in vain; their search was void.
The land they scoured full many a mile:
"Lisle without clocks; clocks without lisle."
Such was their melancholy news,
But Rumford still disdained to choose.

Instead, he bellowed, turning crimson,
"Count me with 'Sockless Jerry' Simpson!"*

*Populist Party leader, and U.S. congressman from Kansas in the last decade
of the 19th Century. He would have been known to Bullock, whose wife
was American and who had several times visited the United States.

Gresham Kohler

If one encountered Gresham Kohler
In his accustomed raven bowler,
Umbrella on his arm furled tightly,
Starched cuffs and collar gleaming whitely,
Cravat of rich yet chaste selection,
And morning coat cut to perfection,
One would have thought him from The City,
En route to sit on some committee
That had to do with interest ceilings
Or mortgage rates or kindred dealings.
The fact is, he had no substantial
Influence in affairs financial.
Appearance should not be relied on:
He ran a cockle-stand in Croydon.

Trevor Kurtz

The Dorset dandy, Trevor Kurtz,
Was noted for distinctive shirts.
They ranged in hue from mauve to peach,
And never knew the touch of bleach.
Their sleeves were cut like leg o' muttons,
And boasted triple gauntlet buttons.

Alas! Whilst Trevor was away
With yachting friends at Caswell Bay,
Armed with an axe, a wicked child
Broke in, and went completely wild.
(The deed, observed Inspector Horne,
Bore all the marks of *Abercorn.*)

His servant bringing up the rear,
Trevor sustained a shock severe
When he returned to find his door
Ajar and smashed, and on the floor

cont. over ☛

His lovely shirts a reeking blur,
Spattered with ink, smeared with ordure.

It was too much. He could not speak
But uttered an ungodly shriek,
And then collapsed. The police were called.
When they arrived, they were appalled
To find his dusky servant, Ned,
Intoning: "*Mistah Kurtz - he dead.*"*

*A line from Joseph Conrad's novel, *Heart of Darkness*, used by
T. S. Eliot as part of the epigraph to "The Hollow Men".

Lambert Lord

It was the goal of Lambert Lord
To wear a glass without a cord.
Enamored of the Prussian mode,
He thought it great éclat bestowed.
For hours each morning, he would try
To keep one anchored in his eye,
Yet after seconds, truth to tell,
In every case, it always fell.
Concluding that his lack of skill
Must be a defect of the will,
He then resigned himself, alas,
To fix a ribbon to his glass!

Isabel McCall

The hair of Isabel McCall
Was lengthened by an ample fall,
And furthermore, not only that –
Augmented by a massive rat.
If the rat ran and the fall fell,
Not much would remain of Isabel.

The Marchioness of Mal de Mer

The Marchioness of Mal de Mer
Sat rigid in her crested chair.
Beneath her marcelled, blue-rinsed hair,
She stared a basilisk-like stare.

Above her brow, a livid vein
Throbbed like the beat of one insane.
With trembling fingers bent with pain,
She clutched the handle of her cane.

A greenish pallor tinged her face,
All twisted in a grim grimace.
From her clenched lips, a tiny trace
Of spittle dribbled on her lace.

Was it an apparition there
Elicited that ghastly stare?
Fear of the Pit? Remorse? Despair
That gripped the Lady Mal de Mer?

Was it a spectre of the night
That turned her knuckles chalky-white?
Not so: The Lady looked a fright
Because *her corset was too tight*.

Murgatroyd Marsh

This is the story of Murgatroyd Marsh,
Who could not abide any clothes that were harsh,
So readily bruised and so tender his skin
That the slightest abrasion tormented like sin.

He wore linen in Springtime and cashmere in Fall,
With a view to not feeling his clothing at all.
In Summer his garments were cambric and silk,
As soft as a zephyr and soothing as milk.
In Winter he never emerged from his door,
So a nightshirt of flannel was all that he wore.

Yet he died just a score of years after his birth:
Such a sensitive creature was not for this earth.

Montressor Meeks

An aesthete named Montressor Meeks
Was troubled by his sunken cheeks.
He looked as though his teeth were gone,
Although, in fact, they'd not been drawn.
To give his cheeks a rounded puff,
He started packing them with snuff.
Although it did succeed – alas,
This stratagem could never pass!
It, sadly, tended to produce
A copious flow of brownish juice:
He dared not spit; he dared not drool;
He dared not let it form a pool,
Lest he be thought uncivilised,
And by Society despised.
Desisting, he exclaimed: "God's truth!
"Much better sunken than uncouth!"

Miss Myra Micklewhite

Miss Myra Micklewhite, for starters,
Incinerated all her garters.
Then girdles, corsets, belts and sashes,
She likewise soon reduced to ashes.
If asked, she would have told the nation
That such things hamper circulation.
And so her bosoms, flopping limply –
Her abdomen, protruding blimply–
Her stockings, 'round her ankles sagging –
Produced a sight that set men gagging.

Guy Nye

From the breast-pocket of Guy Nye,
Four points precisely one-inch high
Of cambric, edges all hand-rolled,
Protruded, perfect in each fold.
For such effect, fastidious Guy
Was not content to trust his eye,
But rather, to achieve the trick,
Relied upon his measuring-stick.
Once, when the stick had been misplaced,
He was afraid he'd be disgraced
If anyone of taste should spy
His points the slightest bit awry;
And so he kept himself house-bound
For near a month till it was found.

Oliver Arlington Orr

The trousers of Oliver Arlington Orr
Either scarce reached his ankles or dragged on the floor.
He lived all alone in a house near the shore.
His hands were arthritic; his fingers were sore;
And adjusting his braces he found such a chore
That he left them unchanged as they came from the store.
Hence the trousers of Oliver Arlington Orr
Either scarce reached his ankles or dragged on the floor.

Lord Popinjay

On blazer, trousers, shirt and vest,
The buttons of Lord Popinjay
Were all emblazoned with his crest,
So as his lineage to display:
They made a glittering array.

A stick-pin just below the throat
Was sported by Lord Battledore.
Though t'was no bigger than a groat,
His multi-quartered arms it bore
In gules and argent, vair and or.*

Espying which, Lord Popinjay,
Whose arms no quarterings could boast,
Was filled with envy and dismay.
On laudanum he overdosed,
And very soon gave up the ghost.

*In Norman French, the language of heraldry, gules is the term for red; argent and
or for silver and gold, respectively; and vair, for a certain type of fur. The terms
also designate the hatchings used to represent the respective colour, metals, or fur.

Peter Pound

The humble dustman, Peter Pound,
Wore a white boater all year 'round;
But what was more appalling yet,
Its grosgrain band was a duet
Of stripes in lavender and cream –
The colours of a polo team
That lowly Peter and his kind
By no means ever could have joined.
Eventually, the word was spread
That he, who laboured for his bread,
Was guilty of impersonation,
Assuming airs above his station.
E'er long, good Peter's duties put
Such talk to rest, for grime and soot
Made hat and band alike turn black,
And saved him, doubtless, from the sack.

Cyril Pratt

One never noticed Cyril Pratt
Without his Irish walking hat.
Regardless of the day or date,
It always rested on his pate.
From church and chapel both he shrank,
And persons of exalted rank,
And ladies' company eschewed
Lest he might, covered, be thought rude.
His head was free of wen or scar;
Its shape was nothing singular.
With ample hair he was endowed,
Of which most men would be quite proud.
Just why he held in such esteem
The walking hat, no-one could dream:
Of Irish, he had no degree
Within his genealogy,
And as for walking anywhere,
Gout kept him 'prisoned in his chair.

Miss Pringle

Was it the tintype of some cavalier
Enclosed within her garnet-crusted lavaliere?
A handsome swain from out her girlish past,
Between her bosoms in the case held fast?
Consumed with curiosity, her cousins pried
The locket open when Miss Pringle died –
And beheld Bonar Law* enthroned in glory:
The lady was a dedicated Tory.

*Andrew Bonar Law (Conservative) was British prime minister,
1922-23. He resigned because of ill-health after little more
than half a year in office, and died a few months later.

Major Houghton Reid

The gallant Major Houghton Reid
Was passionately fond of tweed.
Cheviot, Harris, Donegal –
It mattered not; he loved them all.
For many years, this was his creed:
If mufti, then it *must* be tweed.
But then, one morning on parade,
His brigadier was quite dismayed
To see the major's uniform
Was cut from cloth unlike the norm.
"It's most non-reg," he brusquely barked
When he the major's costume marked.
"Tweed uniforms will never do.
"Remove it, Reid, or I will you!"
The doughty major stood his ground,
Refused the order, and was bound
And stripped alike of brass and braid,
Summarily reduced in grade.
He did not quail. He did not flinch.
He did not yield a single inch.
So he was drummed out of the corps,
To be an officer no more.

Miss Daphne Satterthwaite-Sinclair

Miss Daphne Satterthwaite-Sinclair
Was never certain what to wear.
She might attend the Bishop's tea
In skirts that failed to hide the knee,
Or dress in billowing chiffon
To play at bowls upon the lawn.
Such gaffes drew comment, often snide,
Which reached her ears and hurt her pride,
Till she exclaimed, "The deuce take it!"
And joined the nudists in a snit.

Lady Savile

The knitted frocks of Lady Savile
Were somehow likely to unravel.
She had a tendency to snag them,
And would have done well just to bag them.
Once, promenading after sherry
In Regent's Park as customary,
She caught her hem on a projection,
Which quite eluded her detection.
She leisurely her walk concluded,
The while, progressively denuded,
So, when she'd finished with her stroll,
She stood in shift and camisole.

Maud Saunders

It was Maud Saunders' fond conceit
That through the years she'd stayed petite,
When actually, as time went by,
The pounds began to multiply.
Whene'er she tried on a new frock,
She would encounter a fresh shock,
Yet never once did it occur
That the fault really lay in her.
Instead, indignant, she'd maintain
That, ever seeking greater gain,
The manufacturing enterprises,
To save on cloth, had changed the sizes.

Arabella Shand

The glittering Arabella Shand
Had always fork or spoon in hand:
She knew that gloves are never worn
    Whilst eating, by the gentle-born,
So ate *sans* pause, as one hag-ridden,
To keep her rings from being hidden.

Sukie Simpkins

Since Sukie Simpkins always wore
A ruffled gingham pinafore,
The other girls at Ravenshead
Wore linen pinafores instead.
Though she was comely, kind, and bright,
With manners fetching and polite,
They kept their dress from hers distinct
For fear they might with her be linked
In someone's mind, and thus unmade.
You see, her father was *in trade*.

Merrill Moffat Sloane

When death took Merrill Moffat Sloane,
His body weighed full thirty stone.*
Regardless how they tried to fold him,
No coffin ready-made could hold him.
They dared not wait to custom-fit him,
For fear that first the worms would get him.
So into ash they rendered Merrill,
With grease enough for half a barrel.

*Stone: A British unit of measurement equivalent to 14 pounds avoirdupois.

Wilfred Snell

It was the whim of Wilfred Snell
To sport a flower in his lapel,
Which would have passed upon the street
As being just a bit effete,
And yet undoubtedly embraced
Within the boundaries of good taste,
Had Wilfred only been content
With modest floral ornament.
A small carnation, none could fault;
Or rosebud violently assault
Propriety, and yet such blooms
He thought as boring as legumes.
Instead, upon his chest one spied
A full-grown tulip in its pride,
Or, as he strolled in Picadilly,
A peony or calla lily,
Which, all agreed, seemed rather queer
And bulky for a boutonniere.

Miss Gillian Snipes

The corpulent Miss Gillian Snipes
Was not entirely clear on stripes.
She'd heard couturières advise
That vertical would slenderize,
Whilst horizontal should be shunned
By all whose figures are rotund.
Yet, though she tried, there was a hitch:
She kept forgetting which was which.
So she decided over tea
That she'd renounce them equally.

Claude Speight

It caused a scandal when Claude Speight
Appeared in brown well after eight
One evening - (Just imagine, brown,
Not in the country but *in town*),
Which undercut and overran
His claim to be a gentleman.

Mrs Basil Swope

Bejewelled Mrs Basil Swope
Was greatly envious of the Pope:
"How cruel!" she thought. "Restricted, I'm,
"To one tiara at a time,
"Whereas I understand that he,
"In full pontificals, flaunts *Three*.

Thomas Tinkham Tattersall

Young Thomas Tinkham Tattersall
Was heedless, oft, of Nature's call.
His Dad, contemptuous and unhappy,
Demanded that he wear a nappie* –
Which were as normal as might be,
Had Thomas not been *an MP.***

*A diaper.
**A Member of Parliament.

George Tilton

Before George Tilton's uncle died,
He called the young man to his side.
"Take this, and use it well," he said,
"To 'mind you of me when I'm dead,"
And handed him a tiny case
From which ingenious resting-place
Toothpick and earspoon both did fold;
And all was made of solid gold.
It was not George's first intent
To employ either instrument
In public, but there came a time
When he concluded it a crime
That precious items such as they
Should not be subject to display,
And finally, as fitly due them,
He had a nosepick added to them,
Wielding all three with ostentation
From Charing Cross to Euston Station.

Carlos Urrutía

The Spaniard, Carlos Urrutia,
Had a bad case of seborrhea
Which left him fairly mantled daily
With dingy dandruff, dull and scaly.
Though others eyed it with great loathing,
He would not brush it from his clothing –
In fact, a navy coat affected,
That it might better be detected.
"It makes me think," he told beholders,
"Of lovely snowflakes on my shoulders."

Grandmère Voisin

Grandmère Voisin was fond of jabots.
She always wore them with her sabots.
No-one would tell her to her face
That wooden shoes looked gauche with lace.

Giles Ward

Giles Ward, residing near Balmoral,
Had hair a vivid shade of coral.
It was assumed that he had dyed it,
And he had not, in fact, denied it.
Some true well-wishers sought to guide him,
And gently undertook to chide him:
They said, "It looks so artificial,
"The impact could be prejudicial.
"Grey is august; can't you perceive it?
"Why not let it grow out, and leave it?"
"Dear Friends," he answered, pale and shaken,
"Your supposition is mistaken.
"If only some benignant wizard
"Could render me a perfect grizzard,
"With grey locks I should not be gladder.
"Alack! Their natural hue is madder."

Percy Weld

It was the wont of Percy Weld
To wear his shirts until they smelled.
"Since washing causes them to fray,"
He said, "I make them last this way."
"Well then," exclaimed his Cousin Prue,
"Why not your drawers and singlets, too?"
His answer drove her up the wall:
"Because I don't wear *them* at all."

Norbert West

One thing distinguished Norbert West:
White linen piping on his vest.
A time arrived when even fops
Could not find piping in the shops,
So Norbert took a pair of snips,
And cut his table cloth in strips.

Roland Washburn White

At forty, Roland Washburn White
Had still not mastered left and right.
Whenever he had suits bespoke,
He'd always mumble, cough, and choke,
And for an answer be hard-pressed
When asked to tell which way he dressed.*
Assuming Roland to be shy,
His tailor (disinclined to pry)
Just cut his trousers extra-wide
With ample room on either side.

*"Do you dress to the left or to the right, Sir?" is a euphemism employed by British tailors when measuring gentlemen for trousers. More detailed explanation here would be unseemly, and, one ventures to hope, should not be necessary.